In the Long Ago

Samuel J. Boardman

Copyright
December 2015
Des Moines, Iowa

An Offering:

Grandma had her roux, a kind of sweet spot most athletes know about when the bat and ball meet in heavenly combustion and the cowhide sphere takes off into the place of kites, fire-flies, and dreams.

 I would guess most of us seek the essence of our days. At least, I know I do. And it really doesn't matter if we are deliberate in this. For, it's a bit like trying to hide from your dog—if you love him, and he loves you—he will find you. There's a sweet spot; a measure of roux waiting for us all.

This book is my roux, my medicine, and its potency is realized only when it is shared.

 Grandma was pleased when she found the roux in her gravy, but she was over-joyed when she presented that taste to her family.

<u>In the Long Ago</u> is a staff to keep me balanced between the past and the present; a leaning post, and, perhaps a learning post between the root-ball and the tree. It's the taste I offer to you.

Each of the offerings I have presented on these pages has brought me pleasure, and as these words, thoughts, and images intersect with those of you who read them, my pleasure will turn to joy.

A Breath...

It is time to take a breath and realize how fortunate I am to have the family of angels who have patted me on the back, smiled in my direction, and cheered me on in the midst of the mining of this material. I thank you all. This book has never been intended as a vanity piece---this is not a jog down ego lane. Your friendship and encouragement have bolstered the journey. Thank you to all, especially, my friend, Byron. "Here's to you all!"

Contents

The Bozo Light   7

The Plug   9
Slip of the Moon   11
They Never Told Me   13
Fruit Trees   14
The Loon's Doxology   15
The Park   16
Now Waits   18
Prairie Path   19
Blue Chair   20
Walking Us   21
Laid By   22
Waiting   24
Metamorphosis   26
Embraced   27
Dust Up   29
Checking In   30
Curandera   32
Paying Attention   33
Good-bye   36
Elder   37

The Feeding Field   38

Gun Lap   41
Chalk   43
Fine   45
Ashes to Ashes   46
Instead   47
Impossible   48
Quiet Hands   49
Hold On   50

In the Long Ago   51
The Sax   52
Greeting Bone   54
Noun   55
Jammin' with Eternity   56
Reframe   58
π   60
Earth Child   61
The Shaman   62
Water Breaks   64
The Monk's Living Room   65
Sacred Places   67

Home   69

Upheaval: For Adults Only   72

.333   74

The Bozo Light

Lying in bed with my Bozo night light as my great protector was not exactly the most secure I had ever felt. The dark of my bedroom seemed to be more of a cover that kept me from having to face the confusion and challenges life had slipped under my door, uninvited. I suppose I ought to have been grateful for the evidence of Bozo's red nose, revealing both a portion of light, and my parent's concern that I would not be left entirely alone, to fend off whatever lurked in darkened corners of the room or my mind.

Of course, now I realize there is an infinite cadre of opponents and adversaries lying in wait in the folds of the gray matter of my brain, more than there ever was in that room of my childhood long ago, when Bozo was my only light.

What are the memories that cling to us like unwanted cobwebs? They hold to us like urchins, fearful of being abandoned, yet knowing they must join the grist of the past.

I recall reading somewhere that at the moment the teeth of a cat break the skin of its prey hanging helplessly from its mouth, a form of natural novocaine streams through the victim's body relieving the bird, mouse, or rabbit of pain, numbing---shutting down all body systems---and then, mercifully dying.

I don't know if this is true, but I do know that childhood bruises and cuts still hurt, if only in memory. And the canine incisors that penetrated my back-side, as I ran from him, are still very much felt.

What is it about reaching a plateau in our lives and being unable to return to moments when climbing out on a limb, walking through narrow clinging passage ways, scrambling over hills, walking across frozen creeks, and stooping in narrow passage ways, were of no consequence?

Time brings with it caution, and the burden of safety at all costs. Why not swing from the branch and lithely bounce on to the earth? Why does the cushion now become an obstruction to adventure, a brute force intending to break our spirit, if not our bones?

Wisdom, we answer! Yes, but where is the playful risk? Where is the carnival aspect of joy?

Even with the clown's nose providing a presence, there still were shadows, shapes insistent upon changing and forming images that would drive me deeper under the covers. In those moments of confrontation, with novice wisdom, I sought to swing from the branch; to lithely bounce to the earth. I did not call out to my parents, to break through the dark and my fear.

I heard another voice, "Burrow in, lie still, and close your eyes. Tomorrow will come, and Bozo will be just another silly, wonderful clown."

As I think about the little spit of light coming from the red nose of that plastic figure staring at me from across the room, I am reminded of the light houses, prominently placed, so that ships will see themselves safely through the dark. Tomorrows do come---always with another opportunity for us to figure this all out.

The Plug

I was three as she knelt easing me into the water.
The buttery summer sun brightened the walls
of the cubbyhole bathroom.

Her hand kept me upright
in the porcelain tub with the funny legs.
The other hand deftly washed off diaper mishaps
and evidence of an active boy claiming his place
in the world.

Between wiggles, giggles, and the plopping
of my little duck in the warm slippery water,
I missed seeing her pull the plug.

She let go of me!...my jabber stopped....

The toy duck, caught in the swift current,
moved rapidly toward the sinkhole.
My bottom slid easily on the smooth surface
pulling me toward the gaping mouth.

Now I join my Gaelic ancestors keening and looking
for those who do not scuff happy endings;
a story teller who has seen the faces of yearning
for no more skinned knees or bloodied messages,

a man who is beginning to see that neither the
duck nor I went down with the swirling
soapy water---a lesson is inching its way
forward---

an elder cuts his teeth on sorrow and sharpens
his skills on disappointments.
So pull the plug mom! Let me go.

Hoorah and hurray! Join Alice's rabbit...
go through the hole;
put pontoon wings on childhood tubs
and say, "Thanks mom, for pulling the plug."

Slip of the Moon

Doughnuts, in a church
parking lot, with a teenager,
wasn't exactly on my bucket list.

With no one stirring,
the car broke through a pristine
blanket of snow.

Before giving over the reigns
I took us for a buggy ride.
The nose of the car slapped
and slipped over the quiet bed.
The doughnuts were exquisite!

Though the car slinked and slid
because the lot was large and empty
it was fun—not dangerous.

Now, as my car eased its way
to an empty parking lot...no snow;
without an anxious daughter
preparing for a rite of passage---
the driver's exam,

the doughnut day of the winter past
came to mind. I was facing
my own exam...first big meeting
with my new congregation.

With heart rhythms in overdrive,
and unwanted visitors in my
stomach, I made my way to the door.

"You've done your work; allow me to do mine."
A voice, offering these words;
just as I looked up into the slate
gray sky, seeing the slip
of the moon....

"Dad, I don't know if I am ready..."

My daughter's voice came to mind,
even as I was wondering the same
for me.

As I walked toward the door,
looking at the moon, I smiled...
hearing the voice---

"Let me do the rest."

They Never Told Me

They never told me about
shiny drains pulling babies
down waiting mouths

They never told me about
fathers with heavy wild hands

They never told me about
letters and numbers crawling
into everything but my brain

They never told me
little babies coo and cuddle
grow up and carry their parents
in faded memories and dreams

They never told me
I do sometimes means I don't
and I will when I won't

Fruit Trees

My dad grew better trees in
his little south forty than sons.

The earth rolled over and showed
her belly when he scratched
her open and planted his trees:
pears, apples, and peaches.

From their branches sprang
glorious fruit.

My brother and I...our roots
seemed not to take hold.
We didn't stay put. We grew
every which way....

He wasn't around to see the blossoms
or, pick the fruit.

The Loons' Doxology

Loons call...

The uneasiness of a new page:
our welcome delivered by an impudent
mosquito, engaging in a transfusion,
unwanted.

To reciprocate, a flip of the hand...
a red smear appears on the window---
vacation has begun.

Moments carefully woven together
birthing memories....

Stepping in and stepping out
of nature's delights:
lakes, stalwart pines, a black bear,
a wolf, along the highway---reminding
us of the unsettled question:
Whose land is this?

Ojibwa, pioneers, immigrants---leaving
their spirit in the midst of our recreation;

our time of re-birth, with periodic squalls,
uproars like brief seizures; small
fissures in the magnificent rock,
called family.

And finally, the loons' doxology---
sending us home.

The Park

I needed to see the park.
This time from an ethereal distance
with my head on straight, and my heart
beating the Blues.

I had known of this green patch
and how the neighborhood had endured
keeping it a safe and beautiful place.

Even the grass and trees, in an unquiet state,
want to hear laughter and sounds of silliness
children conjure up; not cacophony:
anxious parents, frustrated angry youth...
the young ones caught in between.

From its inception, the intent was to have
An Elysian field and not Flanders. If tears
were to be shed, let them be about skinned
knees, sunburns, and mosquito bites.

Let the memories of those who play, over-see,
relax, be not held in fear---and may their stories
be sweet to the lips, and joyously conveyed.

I had come to the park to tell stories;
I ended up receiving one.
The staff were cordial; the kids, curious,
flighty, rambunctious...and wonderful!
Roaming from table to table, cluster to cluster,
at least two, three, children wanted to hear
my stories.

The ripple drew others to listen.
After moving about like a bard with a decided
shuffle, I landed on a bench and stayed put.

One small boy kept saying, "Tell another."
More children joined us: Some playing
with a puzzle; some sitting, gazing at me,
"Tell another."

All listening to a story, that for a few clicks,
took us to a different place and time.
"Tell another", and so I did.

Now Waits

The harvest is in.
The land has given its treasures
and now waits the resting time.

It's been twelve seasons, the little
corner of authenticity has hung
out its sign; the people have come.

The people have entered the story
where they can. They are the broken
bread shared...the harvest is in....

Prairie Path

Prairie grass brushes our legs like a pony's tail;
dragon fly flits through the air.

Blue stem and switch grass spread
before us; memories of moccasins
walking this land.

From the path cut and smoothly trod
shagbark waits.
Grandmothers disguised as aging oaks
stand as a chorus of welcome and blessing.

Big and blue bend in the slight breeze
teetering but never falling.
Our senses on overload—
momentarily disquieted.

Tops of yellow cone flower and turkey foot
lift my eyes to the azure sky.

The winged visitor soaring in the distance
shapes the moment...hawk.

The field mice scurry through the baptisia,
disappearing, like the stand of prairie smoke
so evident in June.

Blue Chair

Yesterday I sat in a blue chair
images of a young woman arose
like prairie smoke swiftly dissolving
into poetry

I saw you

I saw a nimbus above your head
and a birth of memories dueling
with tears

I come to you as a whisper
entering your thoughts
like an angel on tip toe

bearing a gentling compassion
listening for a message
from the dawn

Walking Us

We walk through the prairie
in single file. The winds blow---
the grassland rattles its greeting.
The hawk circles...swoops like
a child's kite above our heads.

An oasis...a snatched parcel...
now for recreation.
An escape from well-ordered
manicured lives, has become
a sacred space.

The path twists gently,
propelling us toward meadow
and open field.
We walk in silence, except
for the murmuring of long ago
souls, flowing together
with the swaying grass
and our careful steps.

The Hawk watches....
A dog barks from a nearby farm.
The path walks us now;
carrying us out of the prairie
to the meadow, and the hill,
where the grandmothers
in the guise of ancient oaks,
bid us---come.

Laid By

Crops are laid by---milkin's done;
night claims tired bones.
Time for ponderin and thankin the good Lord;
though there ain't been much---in a human way of thinkin.

Sittin with these folks brings an ease to me.
They are familiar.
My feet lay easy under their table.

Piety comes through their pores.
They sit comfortably in simplicity;
revealin a road, from the farm to the city
and from the good book, to a blessed life.

No airs---accessible, God-fearin, decent folk.
Good raisin broke through---reached them.
The faucet of scarcity was a lamp, leadin them;
remindin them, shadows always   hold light.

They be parents, educators, family folk; devoted
to human community: widenin the door---
settin one more place at the table.

Slips from their hearts planted in lives along the way. Common sense folk---kind, seasoned with stripes, to prove it.

Count on people, wantin decisions
dipped in gospel actions, circled in grace;
not as a demand, but a heart's desire.

Crops are laid by---milkin's done.
The night claims tired bones---
time for ponderin and thankin
the good Lord.

Waiting

The old dog walks across the spring grass
a branch from the maple tree lies in his path---
he stumbles.
Seizures topple him; his leg churns,
one paw reaching beyond the other
like a puppy running across the field.
A pilgrimage; not a romp.
A journey, beyond grass and sunny days---
beyond abhorrent miss-firings
of brain synapses.

The country boy plays his guitar, grateful
his fingers find their place on the strings
as his mind seeks exit.
Music---memories: memories awash
like clothes pins with no line.
His star fading---fans' applause stored
on last year's calendar---stardom locked
in a cranial prison.

Each waits....

They wander, get lost in corners;
depend on others to keep them safe.

A small brown rabbit remains still.
The venerable gray beard neither sees
nor picks up the scent.

The celebrity and the canine
swept into a mental cage,
distorting gift and instinct,
pulling them away from today
to the tapestry of tomorrow,
tomorrow and tomorrow.

Each has left his mark,
the brave country troubadour
and the amiable dog from KC.

The dog with the lion's head and soft
bovine eyes slips away---his life-line
severed---he is still.

The guitar man---waits.

Metamorphosis

I sit against the gnarled old maple
gazing through the branches to see you
hung so perfectly in the sky.

You look as you appeared seventy
years ago. I stood near the mesh
screen waiting my turn at home plate,
as the bubble I blew in anticipation
of driving the ball in your direction
momentarily blocked you from view.

If I stood on Gorky Street, strolled
the Champs-Elysees, or leisurely
walked old Division, leading past
my boyhood home, I would know you.

You have the same glint and girth,
while my reach has lessened;
my sight as well. There is gray in
my grizzle, and a hitch in my step.

The cockroach continues to dance,
while I and my old dog keep rhythm
to a toothless piano, missing the beat.

The monarch and the tiger swallowtail
flit and flutter on thermal lift,
landing gently on lupine and peony.

Children in the park climb with alacrity,
the slide shaped like a dragon,
and flow down its big red tongue.

I sit and marvel.

Embraced

The grandmothers bent to cradle him;
running as he had as a puppy, the miniature
grey fellow with the elder's beard loped
like a playful fawn, instead of an ageing canine
with painful joints and clouded sight.

The knoll, with hallowed burr oaks
standing like stalwart guardians,
was not the Elysian Fields; rather a simple
meadow, splendidly lush, with uneven
interruptions...patches of indian grass dotted with
asters and black-eyed susans.

It was a place of picnics for those wearing jeans
and blue denim work shirts.

The dog was the compass my eyes followed;
taking in a sturdy presence of three trees
quietly waiting...

he who limped, now flowed across the grassy hill
and with a jubilant little jump, was enveloped
by the arms of the grandmothers.

Stepping into the moon's foot print, I saw
their luminance---sentient beings; not trunks,
bark, or branches.

Women, beautiful hair of the raven---
skin of pipestone. The grandmothers---proprietors
of the land.

The small gray beard uttered not a sound...
The old ones knelt...he leaped, and they were gone.

Dust Up

The wind blows,
threatening to knock her down,
push her aside.
She is anchored with conviction,
bolstered by life's journal
showing well-worn pages.

While her husband grows fragile,
his body like an infant's hand;
trying to scoop water with
splayed fingers,
she finds ways to keep going.

This woman who, at thirteen, rode herd
on her father's cattle and toughed
out the Kansas prairie,
now faces a trail calling for wisdom
beyond a young girl riding solitary,
looking for lost animals.

Wisdom comes on ancient tributaries
bearing messages; urging her
to stand with the winds.

Decades past when her father's
confidence ran through her blood,
she rode across the creek heading
toward the canyon; the winds dusting up.

Not a sage, but a confident youth,
who saw etched in the stone
lettered evidence, none of us are ever alone.

Checking In

For days I unearthed spaces, slots, shelves.
Repeating myself, I took the tour
several more times.
My heart, dabbling in a cantankerous pool
of memory---frustration and anger growing.

It was a book! One among many of the magma
lying hither and thither about the house.
No little cairns piled neatly;
steering me to its hidden cubby.

Yes, a book, about a depressed poet!
She was privy to the drill;
having walked the frustrated path.

Maybe one who skirts the edge
ought to let the search go.

When did things, objects,
become so important they need
to check in with us?
It wasn't the book---it was the woman
I needed. She had died....

For years, she had been
a room-mate with depression.
Then, one day...cancer. Like the moon
and the sun slipping into a dark cave;
bringing to her a twin, coming unannounced
and without ceremony---
planning to stay for the duration.

This poet had credibility.
I needed to peel the skin away
from my machinations, and piss-ant concerns,
and sit at her feet.

She was my docent, a good woman.
I hated the thought that the moon
and her partner had slipped out.

I found the book when I wasn't looking for it.
Like the old one, who slips away from public
tears and good-byes, the poet was leading
me gently, checking in---soul to soul.

Curandera

I see you little blond girl
You with the big eyes
taking it all in
Sitting in the midst of the flower patch
smiling sometimes   weeping others

Always you return
pushing your fingers   into God's heart
hoping that a seed will cling to you
and you will blossom beyond your own ground

I see you bright one
with questions seeking to tear away the night
always looking   always listening for wisdom

Caretaker   healer   *curandera*
bandage the wounds   quiet the terrors
Diminish your ache   blossom beyond
your own ground   return
pushing your fingers   into God's heart

Paying Attention

I went to the lake to pay my respects to the loons.
The mournful, hypnotic wail had lured me
to the beach.
My family...asleep. I crossed the road to the cobbled
stone path leading to the "loon's estate".

The sun was opening its sleepy eyes
peering through the pines on the far side
of the lake.
I saw nothing but the shadowed pushy movement
of the water---no blacks and whites.

To my left, ten to twenty feet, in this youthful dawn,
a man was raking and shoveling debris
into a barrel strapped to a battered old golf cart.

As I walked the dock, no wider
than a modest coffee table, I steadied
my gait by grasping the metal bars
supporting the bouncy old dock, squawking like a
duck at each of my steps.

Looking across the lake,
there were no celebrity birds
with shiny black tuxedos in sight.

As I turned, gingerly, to return to the beach,
I heard a trill ---a large bird with a white
belly flew in swoops---disappearing over the trees.

"Was that a loon?" I asked the care-taker,
who was scooping the last shovel-full
of twigs, candy wrappers, and empty cartons.

"How should I know; I wasn't paying attention."

This wasn't a quiet moment for him.
It was a time to do his job before the day began.
It wasn't a magic moment, with beauty and wonder
blowing in his ear; tickling him with awe.

He could not stand, mesmerized, forgetting
work schedules, or return to his cabin
to a surly wife and sad-eyed dog.

It wasn't that kind of nature's treat for this man,
nor for me!

As I made my way back to the house on the hill,
I saw him whirling up the road on his battered old
golf cart---probably returning to the surly wife
and sad-eyed dog.

If truth gets a voice here, about the pre-dawn
encounter; neither the green-jeaned one
nor the sophomoric mystic paid attention:
there was no communion....

He didn't see the bird or hear the trill; I
couldn't appreciate the lake, for the lack
of the absentees---neither of us saw the other---
nature and humanity lost that day, in the "loon's
living room".

Good-bye

The birds' wings, tucked and folded,
heard it; the moon, comfortably settled
in the smoky sky, heard it...

Rumbling tires, rolled off the road,
like mama's rolling pin, thumping---bumping
the counter top, flattening the kneaded dough.

Bits of light, flashing over the birds---painful
frightened cries, joining the moon, and the wild-
eyed headlights in the battered fender.

Miles away...in the old hickory night---parents
sleep

as their children chancing the rhythms, and
pushing the seductive envelope---entered the
murky moments of time---not bidden.

Tires rolling, tires spinning---counter top
reverberating---birds...screeching, with distorted
beaks....Bent and twisted metal; broken---
splintered glass...

*the spinning...stops.   The engine sputters to
silence. Mama's moon holds steady...like comforting
hands.*

Elder

Peeking into your life I grow self-conscious
mining your biography.
I enter your life like a reprobate swami
with a cracked crystal ball;
trying to see you; to honor your sojourn.

I wrestle, as did you, with Descartes.
You cut your teeth on his words
and gloried in the existential symphony
of thinkers, and the clear
declaration, "Jesus loves me".

With minimum time spent in your company,
I dare to walk into your biography.
Your mind, a minaret: facile, fascinating,
attracting novices to your door.

I can only guess there are moments you breathe
sweet air of philosophical quandary, and
Socratic deliberation with your charges.

Still, cognitive awareness is a one legged man:
compassion, astuteness, heart,
are as compelling---maybe more so.

Tillich, Barth, Socrates, legging it
in the shadow of the man from Nazareth.
All plucking your heart strings, treading
gently into your biography---finding
home in your soul.

The Feeding Field

When I was a kid it was quite common to be challenged by your buddies, "I dare you." Those were the magic words. Particularly if you were a boy, it was hard not to accept the dare. Every bone in your body shouts, "Take the dare! Take the dare!" And for me that voice is still active. It is the stimulant showing that you are still willing to move off stuck places.

So, when my friend, Bill Terrell, who is also my acupuncturist, invited me to sit in the waiting room and write, soaking up the atmosphere; feeling the energy of the people, I decided to take him up on his offer.

It was December 10, 2013, just one day before my mother's birthday: She would have been 99 years old! Maybe she, or her spirit, nudged me to sit that day in the Acupuncture Clinic; after all, she was a nurse during her life and spent many good hours in a healing center, the Kewanee Public Hospital in Kewanee, Illinois.

Incidentally, both my brother and I were born in that same hospital. So, there I was, sitting with strangers at IAC (Iowa Acupuncture Center). It's necessary to open yourself if you wish to step into the dare and stretch beyond the comfortable and known realms of your life.

 I was among strangers-men and women living different lives; coming from different races and experiences, all in this little microcosmic patch of green earth, off Hickman Avenue in Des Moines,

Iowa. I say this, because it seemed I was sitting in a park with life buzzing around me, and everyone, for a brief space in time, had been brought together for a common purpose---to experience healing. I had already had my time with Bill and the process of opening up the channels of energy, lying in a quiet room for respite and allowing my body to receive without help from me.

I use the word energy advisedly because it is a term that speaks of an intangible quality not to be seen, only to be experienced. When I think of this I imagine us sniffing, trying to find the oxygen; or feeling, moving our hands and fingers, trying to grasp the air. I have seen women spray perfume in the air and then walk into the airborne essence; allowing the fragrance to befriend their whole body.

I had placed myself in a chair up against the wall one or two seats away from another. There was a woman helping her child get a drink, and another standing at the desk speaking with Alisha, and one or two persons walking about: all waiting for Bill or Elizabeth to call their name.

The energy flowing at that moment was different than anything I had ever experienced before. Each person in that room had come at the particular moment, not just because an appointment had been scheduled, but in a larger sense, because the cosmos had deemed it time for all of us to come together. It was synchronicity---the tumblers had once again fallen into place.

Because I was writing at this time, allowing my mind to flow with the words literally leaping on to the page, I was not looking around the room, as I might have, if I too had been waiting for my name to be called. In between the cracks of my sensibility, the activity and voices around me eked into my consciousness, but I gently pushed them aside or took from them necessary juice to be added to my work.

There was a veil we all shared, connecting us, and offering evidence that we were not strangers at all. This small patch of green life was our reminder of civilization. It was not my intention to interject myself but rather to be unobtrusive while breathing in the "perfume"; using it to propel my thought, and fulfill my objective to complete the writing exercise, which was teaching me to trust what was within me, and yearning to come to the light of day.

We were not depending upon one another; we were not notes necessary for music; we were the music, undiscovered. That is, until that moment, when I wrote a small truth, like a friendship bracelet, revealing something about us all. Found within our individual voices, our very being is that which draws us together.

It's only through intent that we see; it's only as I sat quietly, and unnoticed, that I realized the wonder of it all. The moment became a feeding field for glory, as if the animals of all stripes had come to the watering hole. And I, with eyes looking beyond words on a page, celebrated the moment, even though I knew when the people left, and the room grew mute, the energy I had felt would be gone.

The whale slaps its tail and only a faint outline remains on the water's surface...and then, gone. The scents, the voices, the sounds I had heard, all interlaced...gone.

Gun Lap

"I think we'll stay here---plant our roots."

That's what he said after
looking around...surveying the space
getting the lay of the land.

We'll stay here....

They walked through our door
like tumbleweeds looking
to stop and settle,
paeans---custodians of a long life;
well marked in lives each had touched.

Teachers of the plains
bearing elder's wisdom, still drinking
from the trough.

Quiet spoken, bright-eyed
wearing their heritage well.
No glad handers, these---
rather earth-borne

springing from an era, still feeding their vision;
informing their steps, grasping
the freshness of the day.

"We're on our last gun lap."

That's what he said. It wasn't morose
or down-turned, it was honest and bold---
matter of fact---but, not cut and dried.

They welcomed us, like a campfire
drawing us to friendship and story.

As the dawn has come, our elder
has moved on.
We are left with memories
listening up---to the one
who has been there.

Quiet words,
quilted with the slightest
prairie hint, now join our story.

Chalk

We sat in a coffee shop called Celebration.
He drew a cornucopia, its horn spilling holons:
math, physics, chemistry---
each a seed of ingenuity climbing toward the sun.

I couldn't join in his playground of cosines
and tangents---his face animated-his fingers
flying over the page like Picasso.

An equilateral triangle slipped into the center
of two surprised circles-his voice hummed
along, spouting integers and Einstein's shop talk;

powering on to his conclusions; while I lagged
behind, leaving Celebration---body surfing
through time, back to elementary school, 1958.

Standing before a slate board, chalk held
motionless, while my class mates impressed
the teacher---who liked to be impressed.

"Clickety-clackety", their chalk in orbit; landing
and taking off on the board, like a NASA bird-
solving the problem for the whole world to see.

I stood motionless, holding the weight of my
chalk, not daring to turn around.... "So", my friend
said, bringing me back, "There it is!", looking like
he had just painted a Monet. "Do you see it?"

All I saw was a red D on my teacher's grade book
next to my name---Pythagoras was not
sitting on my shoulders.

Fine

He stood barely able to walk.
They asked him how he was feeling,
even as it was evident this old war
horse was near to being scuttled.

They helped him to his chair.
She picked up the pillow, placing it
where his back would rest.

The stories carefully slipped from its well-worn
patterns---she remembered her daddy:
present, steady, solid; not the man gingerly easing
into the chair.

"Oh, I am fine." They didn't argue,
believing what they saw: the stoic
demeanor surprised no one.

This man stepped in time with others
of his generation: sorrow, anguish, fear
kept with a tight lid. Like shadow relatives
never introduced but kept close.

They talked of grand-children, gardens
blossoming, and trips planned.
His gaze was beyond all that.

She "futsied" with his shoe lace, remembering
better days.

From Ashes to Ashes

Looking out the Ashram window
leaves lie heavily on the waiting ground
The large maple leans forward
as if to shake free its dried brown tenants
knowing they will let loose and join
the ones being walked on   raked
and hauled away
As a boy I would kick through the crispy
mounds listening to the sounds
lifting maple oak and elm
watching them
spin
swirl
and fall
waiting for another to hear their voice
before being borne away
From ashes to ashes

Instead

I went looking for blue birds today.
Instead, I encountered a sassy raccoon with
a perfect bandit face.

I sought the stealthy airborne creature
with cerulean wings and russet breast,
but discovered a wild turkey with her tiny brood.

I searched for a spider's stairway;
glistening from bough to earth, and I was pushed
by intrusive branches to steps I would not have
taken.

I went looking for pathways smooth and paved
but found earth-born stones and foot-worn roots.

I went looking for a chapel in the pines
and met a doe who stood in silence…
willing to pray with me.

Impossible

Last night the glass ceiling cracked...
from out of the mouth of a child
came shuddering words: "That's impossible!"

This prodigy of Wynken, Blynken, and Nod
snipped hope, like a ribbon at a grand opening;
only there was no celebration.

The ribbon had become a string,
snapped with little effort.
The request: "Go, capture the wind
in this blue bucket---"

The wind couldn't be seen;
the task, as empty as the bucket---
both hidden, beyond reach, in the child's mind.
Where does the imagination closet itself
when belief stumbles to catch up?

Quiet Hands

At the moment of his passing
she lay crisscross against his chest,
as if protecting a wounded comrade
on the battlefield.

The father she never heard, his hands
like a nubbin on butcher paper,
wrote his wishes with Sign
on to her eyes.
The man whose name she carries is gone;
his hands are still.

Her hands now rest
and hold themselves open
for the light of each day.

Hold On

You come from a place read about in magazines
or an answer on quiz or test from ancient lands.
Where life still holds dust of the past
and blood smeared history links you
across continents and time.

Your strong shoulders and supple mind
have served you; fortunately, quiet
certainty runs through your veins
coming from childhood memories
bringing calm and peace.

Strength is revealed through energy of presence
and with ease, others are drawn to you.

Laughter, like sprinkles on a dairy queen, swirls
across your face---a mental note
appears in the heart of the other:
"Here is one of the good guys."

We all have stories---sometimes, like welcomed
companions, other times, like a log, dragging
our steps and muffling our energy.

Our well runs deep; spirit even deeper,
beyond the hardened ground comes the voice:
Hold on...hold on.

In The Long Ago

Baseball, the first expression
of lived dreams and physical skills,
in the midst of growing bodies, malleable
minds and glorious friendships.

One sip of this cup necessitates another,
and the hunger to see possibility lived out
on field and in truth.

Quenched slightly by hints...dreams
frequently end, like a child's soap bubble
or fool's gold, shining for a time,
then, not so quietly, losing their attraction.

But the thirst for sweaty competition
and mastery of stick and ball holds for the few.

In the long ago, their nectar was consumed.
These young, fresh souls filled with hope;
caught in a myth choreographed in the midst

of horse-hide smells and undying belief-
strike outs will desist and hits will come-
like the seasons.

Their eyes will see the game as more than a sport.
With their natal gift and Arthurian blessing,
they will become the heroes for others living the
dream....

The Sax

In the bright lights of the carnival midway
my toss was true.
The ring hit the edge and circled the peg
for a winner.
"I'll take the sax", I said.

My first horn was shiny gold
in all its plastic glory,
small enough to fit into my palm.
The keys invited my touch,
even if all that came out
was distorted air.

Blues hid in the dark of the horn.
Jazz clamoring to get free!
Notes! Crawling all over,
like rambunctious children
kept in at recess because of rain.

I played a mean sax
when I was young; blowing
some fine, sweet music, but sadly,
only in my head.

Did I say the sax was a toy? It was.
Did I say that I did not know
how to release the notes; •
declare amnesty for the sound?

I was a rocket scientist
with no rockets; a doctor with no
patients, teacher with no students.

I had a horn, but the notes
weren't within its plastic nervous system;
the sound was dime store
not, "Blue Note."

My jazz---My blues---
wants to breathe, to see the light of day.
My jazz... My blues still waits for release.

The Greeting Bone

He did it on his own, collecting the gift
and offering it at the door....

Some dogs run with happy eyes,
lolling tongue, and lithe body.

Propelling toward me, as the key turned,
I heard barking, and I knew I was home.

He arrived at the welcome rug,
then remembered---the bone---

practically running over my wife,
he juked, and raced to the family room
where on his pad, tucked in a neat corner,
nestled the bone---

snatching it, like a boy grabbing
his glove for a catch with dad,
he trotted proudly, bone in mouth,
and with ceremony, dropped it, at my feet.

A Noun

I am not a noun
My mother may have bronzed
my baby shoes after my premier
but I am not restricted

Come and see through the glass
the verb in me and the adjectives
I am awash in the great verb
strutting my stuff shadowed
by glistening adjectives

My bones may be evident in the noun
But my heart and soul are filled
with adjectives and my blood
runs
rich with exclamations
interrogatives

Look at me
Look at me the declarative
Dare to look
The pesky ellipses try to lessen me but
the verb in me steps into the larger space
defying the cocoon

Jammin' with Eternity

A.

It's Saturday on the steps of October.
My cargo sits comfortably behind me,
strapped in like a co-pilot riding shot-gun.

She is listening to teen-age rock-n-roll,
singing along, keeping rhythm with
every beat—even at times going duet

with the radio, lyric for lyric; bringing
a smile to my face and joy to my
old soul.

A three year old and a grandfather.
We are having an outing: "Grandpa,
could I go with you?"...a time, a moment
to spend with her is not to be passed up.

Driving---keen-eyed; keeping in
the lane, stopping at red lights---moving
in and out---with my back-seat maestro
syncopated, as the guitar solo
on the radio soars into musical orbit;
no words...my little song bird humming
on cue, and keeps jamming with the riffs.

The impromptu concert keeps right on.
My wee rock-chick never missing a beat.
She is lost in the music... and it is
wonderful.

The white light around us sharpens my
vision and my delightful songstress lightens the
day's agenda, like an incubator keeping both
of us in tune.
We are few blocks from home---
and grandma....

B.

In the midst of the concert, we pass
another home, where the occupants
don't stay long; don't sing, or keep time
to the music---where joy is clothed in

pain, and the focus is not on the cherub
who is unstrapped, and freed to bolt
through the front door, into grandma's
arms.

The incubator in this house is more
like a hope chest; a locket, a
Native American medicine bag.
This home is replete with endings,
folded into beginnings.

Just as I hear the magic from the little
one's mouth, we pass the home of
loss and good-byes---

just as we are swept up in the white
light of dreams, and larger visions---
we pass the home where the occupants
don't stay long; where joy
is clothed in pain, and endings fold
into beginnings.

Reframe

You've come a long way, woman,
from blue collar sweat, clapboard
houses, and sultry Jesus songs.

The big question: If we had it right,
why does it feel so wrong?
It wasn't honey oozing from the pulpit
moving over your life.

It was tar---
holding things together:
muffling, smothering,
and noxious, without fresh air.

Amazing, don't you think,
how we can look and see
different things: Jesus, meek
and mild, a Lord,
with switch in hand.

Bible words, scratched into our hearts.
Stories stitching our lives together;
prompts, prying open shells.

You came to the Well
yearning to find a newer path,
a seeker surviving the noxious---
carrying a provocative and soul searing
question:
Is there any way we can do this
without the Bible?

Some things die slowly, sister---
like fallen leaves melding with
the earth, awaiting renewal.
As we begin to live, we begin to die.

More than skin sloughs off...
we gain---we lose. We say
good-bye in pain, or reluctant joy.

You were right.
We need a touch stone.

You removed the barbed wire
from the gospel, accepted the
discomfort of your life space
being stitched together.

Now you hear the shells
breaking.
Sister, from your pulpit,
honey pours from your lips.

Those who walk with you
bathe their sorrows,
disappointments, hurts---
in the healing sweetness of your care.

A long way, woman,
from blue collar sweat,
clapboard houses,
and sultry Jesus songs....

A long way, indeed.

π

Pi r squared...
You smile, knowing the coherence
stepping into the clear truth,
you walk the edges of its revelation;
in conversation with this sign,
you walk close.

My friend, confidant of Pi,
you are an intrigue, with beaker
in one hand and trowel in the other,
you set off.

With vision acute, you see a wrench
along the highway and stop.
You see the anguish of native people, and
stop.

A professor, adept at fielding eager students'
questions; an athlete agile enough to scoop
a grounder in the hole....
You do sense the coherence.

The sunflower stands, with her
feet deep in dry Kansas soil---
her face smiling, welcomes you.

Earth Child

The world's serenity hides its seething mask
and the black clouds hovering over the placid
state of things---go unnoticed.

The stars and stripes substantiate its birth
in the bowels of war, and the dancing eyes
and well-scrubbed faces of democracy
are oblivious to the cries.

Tears of the almighty are stained---polluted
because no one has noticed; the earth-child
has become an expendable.

The Shaman

I went there to tell stories.
Instead, I was met with a story.
Those birthed in my imagination,
waiting in the wings,
were put on hold.

Sitting in the room, taking in the ambience,
I saw a woman pushing a man,
wearing a ball cap too large for his head;
snuggling a stuffed dog to his chest.

She rolled him to a corner spot.
The shaman had entered
the state of chrysalis---
he was living into the analogy
while I still slept with the question.

For the next forty-five minutes
my story-mouth railed on while my friend
sat heavily in my conscious.
The philosophy professor, who had wrestled
with the words of Descartes,
and adeptly offered verbal bouquets
of Jesus, skated in my brain.

I remembered the last conversation
I had with him in his home. Now, as I stood
next to them, he spoke not a word
and she was not certain of my last name.

I had sought to regale my audience.
Now, she was nodding; he seemed
to be with me---and elsewhere,
perhaps in the class room, hearing a lecture,
or deliberating with an undergraduate
on some philosophical or political conundrum.

The professor was still my mentor;
though he spoke no words.
The shaman had entered the state of chrysalis.
I could see---he was living into the analogy.
I--- still slept with the question....

Water Breaks

You stand over parchment
like a monk with funneled hand
allowing sand to fall in wheels of awe
and lines of delicate grace

Water breaks   streamlets in brown and blue
enjoined by hues of amber and magenta

Water breaks through scrapes
and   light touches   diverting and holding true

You   in placid state   watch
as the farmer who welcomes the foal
as the sun awaits the unfolding
petals of the rose

Water breaks   streamlets fade
Colors   s l o w l y   yawn   blink
and stay put

The Monk's Living Room

There is a familiarity about this land.
Kinship is palatable, yet with sharp edges,
and grasping fingers.
It's egg-washed with the blood
of miscalculation and malfeasance.

This place is not for children---
the deeper I drive into its welcome,
the stronger I taste its history.

The pine tree would speak,
if time allowed,
the smooth sumac whispers
its secrets to me, but my destination
takes priority.
Resolve watches for
sign posts to Gethsemane.

The man in cowl and robe
stands in the shadow of blue grass,
white fences, and equine flesh---
hiding the bitter taste of wildness
gone mad.

I am anxious, unclear
of my service, and death,
like a burning string of tin cans,
follows me to the monk's living room.

"You, who have passed,
crossing the plane, know my plight.
You, who would not bar the door
to your hermitage, I come to you
with begging bowl.
Fill it! Stay my fear.

Wake up! Open your eyes.
Father, love trumps death; allow me
to sit at your hearth."

The sumac whispers---a slight breeze blows
past the small white cross in front of me---
in the monastery grave yard.

Sacred Places

An elephant stands close
by the sleeping fire
known only by the one
who has prepared the space
on the shelf.

A razor, brush, blades
join the small black carving
with quiet candle holder;
pushing it into a corner.

A Canadian goose rests
on a walnut table---
never thinking of flight---
stuff accumulates near
the resting bird.

She says, "These are my
sacred spaces—you are
every where."

Now, he may not take off
his shoes, or whisper
when he comes upon
a placid woodland stream,

still, he sees the need
for such defined, fenced-off
sacred places...

a make-shift ball diamond
holds memory of childhood
pleasure---lined by
the Spoon River---and is
a sacred place for him.
The curve of her smile,
the nape of her neck,
a warm, soft kiss---is sacred
for him.

The ebony beast and stately
white-gibbed goose marks
the spot---for her.

A rustic hammered-out
rooster   peers across
the living room from
its armoire perch---

The herald, reminding
him---haphazard stacks
of cd's and a limp-legged
bag of candy, equals---
desecration of her sacred
places.

Yet, if he were to leave
this earth, the ziggurats,
cairns---accumulations---
that warm, soft kiss---
would be wedded...to her stuff.

Home

I watched as the foot board of my childhood bed went past me. It was moving day. All my parents' possessions were moving out of the house in the hands and arms of strangers who had come to the auction to get a bargain.

Mom stood on the sidewalk inching herself down toward the final event. Dad was gone and she was recently moved into a nursing home, and me? I was moving to places in mind and heart I didn't much care to visit. My grandfather was a Cardinal fan. He liked Musial, "Stan the Man". Since my Dodgers had all left and gone to Los Angeles, I was a new born Red Bird. Ken Boyer, the mighty third baseman was my favorite.

When I was a boy, I had taken pictures of all the Cardinals and pasted them on the foot board of my bed, placed in positions just as they would have been if they were on the diamond and field.

As I watched the woman carry the foot board by us I could see the imprint where the pictures used to be. My mother saw much more than baseball heroes pasted on a young boy's bed board. She saw a life time pass by; being held by people who had no idea of the sights, sounds, and emotions emanating from each piece carried haphazardly and thrown in the back seat, or a truck bed, and taken away. "Mom, come back here." She had promised if I stopped to visit her friend she would not go near the auction at the house where we all once lived, my boyhood home and the place where she had spent all of her adult life with my father, giving birth to two sons, working as a nurse at the public hospital--- just two hills and a left turn from where we now stood--- and living with a difficult man, who had been challenged by heart and stomach trouble all his married life. Now she was a widow and recently a new resident in a nursing home just a few miles from where she had lived as a young girl growing up on the farm.

Life had abruptly stepped in---it wasn't that we were naïve and believed that our loss, signified by the empty easy chair sitting by a smoking stand, and the absent scent of Prince Albert's smoke wafting in the air, could somehow be side stepped, and we could by-pass this fraternity we all must experience during our life---no more smoke; no more dad. We knew we had to go through all of this---believing we would make it. I kept looking and re-looking at what was happening. Was it real when it seemed so unreal?

She was like a child in primary school, easing her way down the side walk; peeking at the people who were carrying off her memories: dad's juicer, her mix-master---her old reliable Singer Sewing machine...

I looked at my mom, standing just a half a block from our past. She was an old woman, caught up in mystery and grace. Her face, reflecting what she was doing on that side walk---paying homage to the years that were given to her in that house, which she and dad had made into a home for us all. I didn't see despair in her; rather a curiosity—"Who were these people and what were they going to do with our memories?"

Actually, there was a calm about her. I was the one who felt like my life had become like rice paper---how was I going to walk through the rest of my life with the minimum amount of tearing? I watched as well, as the house which had been my home became like dried bones, with little life---emptied of things, hollowed and sitting as it did long ago before any of my people ever came through its doors---
"It's time to go, mom..."

Upheaval: For Adults Only

When I was young
storms were exciting.
I had no history-
no reference for
disaster or tragedy.
It was a fun-house.
Snap! crackle! pop!
Winds were for kites.
Rain was for summer
showers, and electricity
for light.
Tornados hurricanes
nor'easters and
typhoons,
all for telling around
the camp fire.
Parents insulated us-
horror was sealed
away in their caretaker
pants and responsibility
vests.
Fear was not loosened
'til we too reached
the adult stage,
the journey from
naïve to awareness,
like a gentle eddy
to a raging torrent;
from pup tent
to bomb shelter.
The mantle has
been passed.

The caretaker pants
and responsibility
vest are...

For Adults Only!

.333

I have loved baseball since I was a boy. I collected cards, played catch with my dad, and any time I could hook up with a game in the neighborhood, I was there.

One of my first telecasts on the black and white was baseball, with Dizzy Dean, former St. Louis pitcher, and Hall of Famer and his side kick, Pee Wee Reese, the Brooklyn Dodger Captain and Hall of Fame short stop. I played sand-lot, farm league, little league, and Babe Ruth. It was in me, like Cheerios, peanuts, and Pepsi.

So, baseball is in my biographical DNA. Not long ago, I attended an Iowa Cubs game when the Colorado Sky Sox were in town. A group of us got together to be the boys we once were, to re-live those days when we wore the spikes and could rip a single between short and second base, scoring the clinching run.

I was uncertain about going: where would we sit? Would I become over heated and get sick, like I had the time my wife, daughter and I attended a game in Kansas City--- with the Royals up against my Red Sox? The sun drove me to cover. I guzzled cold drink, and tried hard not to get sick like I had the summer before, when I was a tourist in Israel, and traveling to the Dead Sea. A doctor, who was in our group, told me that I probably would be susceptible to over-bearing sun for the rest of my life, after getting so ill in the desert in the holy land.

The sun, reminiscent of my foray in the desert, halted my Sunday at the ball park with my family and my favorite team. I spent the rest of the afternoon in a motel bed, while the women went shopping. "Dad, are you feeling any better?"---and they were off again; while I slipped into a much needed escape from nausea and misery.
It was overcast, rain was hinting that we might be visited--even with the heart-memory of crowd noises: vendors shouting, "Get your cold beer here---peanuts, red-hots!" ---I wrestled, should I go---or not?

It was odd, as much as I am drawn to ball games, I was anxious---not panicked. I wasn't sure about driving, that is, knowing where to go, where to park, and once we all got situated, where would we sit. How much would those seats cost, did I have enough money, and would my legs cramp up after sitting too long on those hard seats, or my back get numb? Oh, and if I had to go to the bathroom, could I be steady enough on my feet (after sitting on those hard seats), and not trip on the stairs and make a fool of myself; never mind the possibility of breaking a bone? And, if all this "noise" from my inner voice was not getting this unnerving stuff across, how about this one---will I be able to remember where my seat is without using my GPS?

All this aside, the most realistic concern was, how will I handle the heat? The forecast indicated a possibility of a dousing later in the afternoon--- maybe nine innings with good friends was a possibility. Still, I did not want the stress of driving so I asked my son-in-law to drive.

We arrived in ample time to find a parking lot a block away from the ball park, (I gratefully reached into my pocket for the money to pay the parking attendant). At this point, I, like my ten year old grandson, was comfortable in knowing that his father knew where the west gate was located (again, I could not disturb my gps in its slumber) and where we were to meet the others.

Though I was cordial and interacted with everyone, once they all finally joined our group next to the ticket booth, inside my head, the cloud of anxiety and uncertainty kept jabbing away.

As the game began, the inner activity would not subside. During the fourth inning, with the home team leading, they had hit two home runs and their starting pitcher seemed to be clicking, my back began to speak to me. I watched as some of our guys got up and went to the rest room and the refreshment stand without any problem---everyone had returned unscathed, not having spilled their drinks, or dropped their hot dogs.

So, I thought, maybe I can do this on my own steady legs and bolstered memory. I gratefully stood a couple of times---ovations, applause for the Cubs. Oh, and relief, for my back, and numb buttocks--- and the burning sensation in my left knee.

It was now the sixth inning. The score was 5 to 1, in favor of the good guys, when it began to rain. The game continued---so did the rain! At this point, there were five rows behind us each having sporadic empty seats. The next thing I knew, my seat mates were "crab-legging" over top of those empty seats, trying to out distance the rain, which now was certainly making a statement.

The ground crew appeared and began unrolling the tarp to protect the infield. Like Peter Pan's shadow, I followed my mates in the same unorthodox manner---one crab leg at a time; never stumbling as I "hurdled" green chair after green chair, until I joined my group.

I was greeted with a slap on the back and a "good for you." I had impressed with my agility and speed as I "crab-legged" to shelter from the rain. Actually, I hadn't given it much thought. I didn't even look, or pay attention to what my friends were doing, I just reacted when they bolted from the rain.

We were now three rows from the wall in back of the stadium. There were no more rows to offer us seating. There was a protective over-hang offering us a pleasant respite from taking nature's bath, and for me to recover from those last few moments of spontaneous gymnastics.

The rain had snuffled the heat, and with the misty downfall, it became quite pleasant. There was even a breeze, reminiscent of a small fan blowing through the quieting rain, creating a refreshment all of us welcomed, for a time. Then the wind shifted and blew the rain into our cubby hole, and with nowhere to go except to stand with the many hundreds of folks under the central roof, my son-in-law and I decided it was time to go.

My grandson had basketball practice later in the afternoon and knowing that in baseball, if the game gets past the fifth inning, it is considered an official game. And if the game is called, then the team leading at the time of the umpire's decision, wins---the good guys were leading. The rain was really making a statement now as it splattered hard on the roof of the stadium. Time to go.

As we walked past the crowd hunkered down, away from the rain, wondering if they too ought to leave, I looked out through an opening, over the Des Moines River in the distance. It looked very much like the rain was going to stay for a while. I teased my grandson, "Are you ready for the duck-thing?" He wrinkled his nose and shrugged. The answer was, "Sure." I could see it in his eyes. It was no big deal to him.

As we walked through the crowd, my cautious self held to the railing as we went down the narrow steps, trying to move along and not create a bottle neck, while still being careful on the slippery steps. It was also important for me to keep my eyes on my son-in-law as he merged with the crowd.

Once outside, we received the whole treatment: my Cub cap was sopped---the bill was like a roof of an old shed draining water down over my glasses. As we walked, I could feel the squishy wet socks pressing against the sides and bottoms of my shoes. I tried to protect my cell phone by putting my hand over my pocket as we moved quickly past the ball park and in the direction of the parking lot.

Again, that irksome voice within my brain, hit me with---"Where is the car? I can't remember where we parked the car!" Fortunately, my son-in-law, like a homing pigeon, led us right to the "little green frog", the Ford Taurus, now all clean and shiny, from the summer rain.

We all jumped in as fast as we could. Although, that seemed silly considering the fact we were all soaked to our underwear. Being quick or deliberate made little difference. "Sorry", Mark said to me, as he got seated and put the car in gear---"we are getting your seats wet." I laughed, "Look at me!" My hat was dripping---running off the visor like water on an old tin roof; my Levis were like a napkin after a cold beer sweat on it.

As we drove out of the parking lot, heading for home, the voice within stopped pestering. I knew who I was, who I was with, and where we were going---home.

Later, we learned the game had not been called off. The rain had stopped and the Sky Sox had tied the game, Lucky for us, the "good guys" pulled it out in the 11th inning---Cubs win! Cubs win! All was well, though. I was in my home and safe.

Who am I kidding? I may no longer be able to hit a curve ball, but I know safety does not manifest itself through bricks and mortar.

Baseball, is the perfect healing charm. Where else can you go one for three---one hit, three trips to the plate---and walk around with a respectable .333 batting average? That's rarified atmosphere. Home. Safe! ---to play another day.